C000196047

Mastering The Air Fryer Appliance:

An Easy-To-Follow Guide To Affordable, Easy, Fast, Crispy, Delicious & Healthy Recipes For Your Air Fryer That Every Family Member Will Love

CLARISSA HEWITT

Copyright © 2021. All rights reserved.

This document is geared towards providing exact and reliable information in regard to the topic and issue covered. The publication is sold with the idea that the publisher is not required to render accounting, officially permitted, or otherwise, qualified services. If advice is necessary, legal or professional, a practiced individual in the profession should be ordered. - From a Declaration of Principles which was accepted and approved equally by a Committee of the American Bar Association and a Committee of Publishers and Associations.

In no way is it legal to reproduce, duplicate, or transmit any part of this document in either electronic means or in printed format. Recording of this publication is strictly prohibited and any storage of this document is not allowed unless with written permission from the publisher. All rights reserved. The information provided herein is stated to be truthful and consistent, in that any liability, in terms of inattention or otherwise, by any usage or abuse of any policies, processes, or directions contained within is the solitary and utter responsibility of the recipient reader.

Under no circumstances will any legal responsibility or blame be held against the publisher for any reparation, damages, or monetary loss due to the information herein, either directly or indirectly. Respective authors own all copyrights not held by the publisher. The information herein is offered for informational purposes solely and is universal as so. The presentation of the information is without contract or any type of guarantee assurance.

Table of Contents

Breakfast Recipes

1. Flavorful Bacon Cups

Preparation Time: 10 minutes

Cooking time: 15 minutes

Servings: 6

Ingredients:

6 bacon slices

6 bread slices

1 scallion, chopped

3 tablespoons green bell pepper, seeded and chopped

6 eggs

2 tablespoons low-fat mayonnaise

Directions:

Preheat the Air fryer to 375 o F and grease 6 cups muffin tin with cooking spray.

Place each bacon slice in a prepared muffin cup.

Cut the bread slices with round cookie cutter and place over the bacon slices.

Top with bell pepper, scallion and mayonnaise evenly and crack 1 egg in each muffin cup.

Place in the Air fryer and cook for about 15 minutes.

Dish out and serve warm.

Nutrition:

Calories: 260, Fat: 18g, Carbohydrates: 6.9g, Sugar: 1.03g, Protein: 16.7g, Sodium: 805mg

2. Crispy Potato Rosti

Preparation Time: 10 minutes

Cooking time: 15 minutes

Servings: 2

Ingredients:

½ pound russet potatoes, peeled and grated roughly

1 tablespoon chives, chopped finely

2 tablespoons shallots, minced

1/8 cup cheddar cheese

3.5 ounces smoked salmon, cut into slices

2 tablespoons sour cream

1 tablespoon olive oil

Salt and black pepper, to taste

Directions:

Preheat the Air fryer to 365 o F and grease a pizza pan with the olive oil.

Mix together potatoes, shallots, chives, cheese, salt and black pepper in a large bowl until well combined.

Transfer the potato mixture into the prepared pizza pan and place in the Air fryer basket.

Cook for about 15 minutes and dish out in a platter.

Cut the potato rosti into wedges and top with smoked salmon slices and sour cream to serve.

Nutrition:

Calories: 327, Fat: 20.2g, Carbohydrates: 23.3g, Sugar: 2.8g, Protein: 15.3g, Sodium: 316mg

Lunch Recipes

3. Mouthwatering Tuna Melts

Preparation time: 15 min

Cooking time: 20 min

Servings: 8

Ingredients:

Salt (1/8 teaspoon)

Onion, chopped (1/3 cup)

Biscuits, refrigerated, flaky layers (16 1/3 ounces)

Tuna, water packed, drained (10 ounces)

Mayonnaise (1/3 cup)

Pepper (1/8 teaspoon)

Cheddar cheese, shredded (4 ounces)

Tomato, chopped

Sour cream

Lettuce, shredded

Directions:

Preheat the air fryer at 325 degrees Fahrenheit.

Mist cooking spray onto a cookie sheet.

Mix tuna with mayonnaise, pepper, salt, and onion.

Separate dough so you have 8 biscuits; press each into 5-inch rounds.

14

Arrange 4 biscuit rounds on the sheet. Fill at the center with tuna mixture before topping with cheese. Cover with the remaining biscuit rounds and press to seal.

Air-fry for fifteen to twenty minutes. Slice each sandwich into halves. Serve each piece topped with lettuce, tomato, and sour cream.

4. Nutrition: Calories 320 Fat 18.0 g Protein 14.0 g Carbohydrates 27.0 g Bacon Wings

Preparation time: 15 min

Cooking time: 1 hr 15 min

Servings: 12

Ingredients:

Bacon strips (12 pieces)

Paprika (1 teaspoon)

Black pepper (1 tablespoon)

Oregano (1 teaspoon)

Chicken wings (12 pieces)

Kosher salt (1 tablespoon)

Brown sugar (1 tablespoon)

Chili powder (1 teaspoon)

Celery sticks

Blue cheese dressing

Directions:

Preheat the air fryer at 325 degrees Fahrenheit.

Mix sugar, salt, chili powder, oregano, pepper, and paprika.

Coat chicken wings with this dry rub.

Wrap a bacon strip around each wing. Arrange wrapped wings in the air fryer basket.

Cook for thirty minutes on each side in the air fryer. Let cool for five minutes.

Serve and enjoy with celery and blue cheese.

Nutrition: Calories 100 Fat 5.0 g Protein 10.0 g Carbohydrates 2.0 g

5. Pepper Pesto Lamb

Preparation time: 15 min

Cooking time: 1 hr 15 min

Servings: 12

Ingredients:

Pesto

Rosemary leaves, fresh (1/4 cup)

Garlic cloves (3 pieces)

Parsley, fresh, packed firmly (3/4 cup)

Mint leaves, fresh (1/4 cup)

Olive oil (2 tablespoons)

Lamb

Red bell peppers, roasted, drained (7 ½ ounces)

Leg of lamb, boneless, rolled (5 pounds)

Seasoning, lemon pepper (2 teaspoons)

Directions:

Preheat the oven at 325 degrees Fahrenheit.

Mix the pesto ingredients in the food processor.

Unroll the lamb and cover the cut side with pesto. Top with roasted peppers before rolling up the lamb and tying with kitchen twine.

Coat lamb with seasoning (lemon pepper) and air-fry for one hour.

Nutrition: Calories 310 Fat 15.0 g Protein 40.0 g Carbohydrates 1.0 g

Poultry Recipes

6. Chicken Flutes with Sour Sauce and Guacamole

Preparation time: 15 minutes

Cooking time: 25 minutes

Servings: 4

Ingredients:

8 wheat cakes

1 large roasted breast

Grated cheese

Sour sauce

Guacamole

Extra virgin olive oil

Directions:

Extend the wheat cakes.

Stuffed with grated cheese and well-roasted chicken breast.

Form the flues and paint with extra virgin olive oil.

Place in batches in the air fryer and select 180 degrees, 5 minutes on each side or until you see the flutes golden.

Serve with sour sauce and guacamole.

Nutrition:

Calories: 325

Fat: 7g

Carbohydrates: 45g

Protein: 13g

Sugar: 7g

Cholesterol: 0mg

7. Spicy Chicken Strips

Preparation time: 5 minutes

Cooking time: 12 minutes

Servings: 5

Ingredients:

1 cup buttermilk

1½ tbsp hot pepper sauce

1 tsp salt

½ tsp black pepper, divided

1 pound boneless and skinless chicken breasts, cut into ¾ inch strips

¾ cup panko breadcrumbs

½ tsp salt

¼ tsp hot pepper, or to taste

1 tbsp olive oil

Directions:

Put the buttermilk, hot sauce, salt and ¼ teaspoon of black pepper in shallow bowl. Add chicken strips and refrigerate for at least two hours. Put breadcrumbs, salt, and the remaining black pepper and hot pepper in another bowl; Add and stir the oil.

Remove the chicken strips from the marinade and discard the marinade. Put the strips, few at the same time, to the crumb mixture. Press the crumbs to the strips to achieve a uniform and firm cover.

Put half of the strips in single layer inside the basket. Cook at a temperature of 350°F for 12 minutes. Cook the rest when the first batch is cooked.

Nutrition:

Calories: 207

Fat: 9g

Carbohydrates: 5g

Protein: 25g

Sugar: 0g

Cholesterol: 0mg

8. Spinach Stuffed Chicken Breasts

Servings: 2

Preparation Time: 15 minutes

Cooking Time: 30 minutes

Ingredients

1 tablespoon olive oil

1¾ ounces fresh spinach

¼ cup ricotta cheese, shredded

2, 4-ouncesskinless, boneless chicken breasts

Salt and ground black pepper, as required

2 tablespoons cheddar cheese, grated

¼ teaspoon paprika

Instructions

In a medium skillet, add the oil over medium heat and cook until heated.

Add the spinach and cook for about 3-4 minutes.

Stir in the ricotta and cook for about 40-60 seconds.

Remove the skillet from heat and set aside to cool.

Cut slits into the chicken breasts about ¼-inch apart but not all the way through.

Stuff each chicken breast with the spinach mixture.

Sprinkle each chicken breast evenly with salt and black pepper and then with cheddar cheese and paprika.

Set the temperature of Air Fryer to 390 degrees F. Grease an Air Fryer basket.

Arrange chicken breasts into the prepared basket in a single layer.

Air Fry for about 20-25 minutes.

Remove from Air Fryer and transfer the chicken breasts onto a serving platter.

Serve hot.

Nutrition:

Calories: 279

Carbohydrate: 2.7g

Protein: 31.4g

Fat: 16g

Sugar: 0.3g

Sodium: 220mg

9. Cheese Stuffed Chicken Breasts

Servings: 4

Preparation Time: 15 minutes

Cooking Time: 15 minutes

Ingredients

2, 8-ouncesskinless, boneless chicken breast fillets

Salt and ground black pepper, as required

4 Brie cheese slices

1 tablespoon fresh chive, minced

4 cured ham slices

Instructions

Cut each chicken fillet in 2 equal-sized pieces.

Carefully, make a slit in each chicken piece horizontally about ¼-inch from the edge.

Open each chicken piece and season with the salt and black pepper.

Place 1 cheese slice in the open area of each chicken piece and sprinkle with chives.

Close the chicken pieces and wrap each one with a ham slice.

Set the temperature of Air Fryer to 355 degrees F. Grease an Air Fryer basket.

Arrange the wrapped chicken pieces into the prepared Air Fryer basket.

Air Fry for about 15 minutes.

Remove from Air Fryer and transfer the chicken fillets onto a serving platter.

Serve hot.

Nutrition:

Calories: 376

Carbohydrate: 1.5g

Protein: 44.5g

Fat: 20.2g

Sugar: 0g

Sodium: 639mg

10. Bacon Wrapped Chicken Breasts

Servings: 4

Preparation Time: 20 minutes

Cooking Time: 23 minutes

Ingredients

1 tablespoon palm sugar

6-7 Fresh basil leaves

2 tablespoons fish sauce

2 tablespoons water

2, 8-ounceschicken breasts, cut each breast in half horizontally

Salt and ground black pepper, as required

12 bacon strips

1½ teaspoon honey

Instructions

In a small heavy-bottomed pan, add palm sugar over medium-low heat and cook for about 2-3 minutes or until caramelized, stirring continuously.

Add the basil, fish sauce and water and stir to combine.

Remove from heat and transfer the sugar mixture into a large bowl.

Sprinkle each chicken breast with salt and black pepper.

Add the chicken pieces in sugar mixture and coat generously.

Refrigerate to marinate for about 4-6 hours.

Set the temperature of Air Fryer to 365 degrees F. Grease an Air Fryer basket.

Wrap each chicken piece with 3 bacon strips.

Coat each piece slightly with honey.

Arrange chicken pieces into the prepared Air Fryer basket.

Air Fry for about 20 minutes, flipping once halfway through.

Remove from Air Fryer and transfer the chicken pieces onto a serving platter.

Serve hot.

Nutrition:

Calories: 365

Carbohydrate: 2.7g

Protein: 30.2g

Fat: 24.8g

Sugar: 2.1g

Sodium: 1300mg

Fish and Seafood Recipes

11. Cajun Style Catfish

Preparation time: 3 minutes

Cooking time: 7 minutes

Servings: 2

Ingredients:

5g of paprika

3g garlic powder

2g onion powder

2g ground dried thyme

1g ground black pepper

1g cayenne pepper

1g dried basil

1g dried oregano

2 catfish fillets (6 oz)

Nonstick Spray Oil

Direction:

Preheat the air fryer for a few minutes. Set the temperature to 175°C.

Mix all seasonings in a bowl.

Cover the fish generously on each side with the dressing mixture.

Spray each side of the fish with oil spray and place it in the preheated air fryer.

Select Marine Food and press Start /Pause.

Remove carefully when you finish cooking and serve on semolina.

Nutrition:

Calories: 228

Fat; 13g

Carbohydrates: 0g

Protein: 20g

Sugar: 0g

Cholesterol: 71mg

12. Tuna Chipotle

Preparation time: 5 minutes

Cooking time: 8 minutes

Servings: 2

Ingredients:

142g tuna

45g chipotle sauce

4 slices of white bread

2 slices of pepper jack cheese

Directions:

Preheat the air fryer set the temperature to 160°C.

Mix the tuna and chipotle until combined.

Spread half of the chipotle tuna mixture on each of the 2 slices of bread.

Add a slice of pepper jack cheese on each and close with the remaining 2 slices of bread, making 2 sandwiches.

Place the sandwiches in the preheated air fryer. Set the timer to 8 minutes.

Cut diagonally and serve.

Nutrition:

Calories: 121

Fat: 4g

Carbohydrates: 2g

Protein: 16g

Sugar: 0g

Cholesterol: 36mg

13. Fish Tacos

Preparation time: 10 minutes

Cooking time: 7 minutes

Servings: 4-5

Ingredients:

454g of tilapia, cut into strips of

38 mm thick

52g yellow cornmeal

1g ground cumin

1g chili powder

2g garlic powder

1g onion powder

3g of salt

1g black pepper

Nonstick Spray Oil

Corn tortillas, to serve

Tartar sauce, to serve

Lime wedges, to serve

Directions:

Cut the tilapia into strips 38 mm thick.

Mix cornmeal and seasonings in a shallow dish.

Cover the fish strips with seasoned cornmeal. Set aside in the fridge.

Preheat the air fryer for 5 minutes. Set the temperature to 170°C.

Sprinkle the fish coated with oil spray and place it in the preheated air fryer.

Put the fish in the air fryer, set the timer to 7 minutes.

Turn the fish halfway through cooking.

Serve the fish in corn tortillas with tartar sauce and a splash of lemon.

Nutrition:

Calories: 108

Fat: 26g

Carbohydrates: 11g

Protein: 9g

Sugar: 0g

Cholesterol: 56mg

Meat Recipes

14. Greek Beef Mix

Preparation time: 5 minutes

Cooking time: 30 minutes

Servings: 4

Ingredients:

2pounds beef stew meat, roughly cubed

1teaspoon coriander, ground

1teaspoon garam masala

1teaspoon cumin, ground

A pinch of salt and black pepper

1cup Greek yogurt

½ teaspoon turmeric powder

DIRECTIONS

In the air fryer's pan, mix the beef with the coriander and the other ingredients, toss and cook at 380 degrees F for 30 minutes.

Divide between plates and serve.

Nutrition: Calories 283, Fat 13, Fiber 3, Carbs 6, Protein 15

15. Beef and Fennel

Preparation time: 5 minutes

Cooking time: 30 minutes

Servings: 4

Ingredients

2pounds beef stew meat, cut into strips

2fennel bulbs, sliced

2tablespoons mustard

A pinch of salt and black pepper

1tablespoon black peppercorns, ground

2tablespoons balsamic vinegar

2tablespoons olive oil

Directions

In the air fryer's pan, mix the beef with the fennel and the other ingredients.

Put the pan in the fryer and cook at 380 degrees for 30 minutes.

Divide everything into bowls and serve.

Nutrition: Calories 283, Fat 13, Fiber 2, Carbs 6, Protein 17

16. Lamb and Eggplant Meatloaf

Preparation time: 5 minutes

Cooking time: 35 minutes

Servings: 4

Ingredients

2pounds lamb stew meat, ground

2eggplants, chopped

1yellow onion, chopped

A pinch of salt and black pepper

½ teaspoon coriander, ground

Cooking spray

2tablespoons cilantro, chopped

1egg

2tablespoons tomato paste

Directions

In a bowl, mix the lamb with the eggplants of the ingredients except the cooking spray and stir.

Grease a loaf pan that fits the air fryer with the cooking spray, add the mix and shape the meatloaf.

Put the pan in the air fryer and cook at 380 degrees F for 35 minutes.

Slice and serve with a side salad.

Nutrition: Calories 263, Fat 12, Fiber 3, Carbs 6, Protein 15

Side Dish Recipes

17. Baked Sweet Potatoes

Preparation time: 10 minutes

Cooking time: 10 minutes

Servings: 2

Ingredients:

2 big sweet potatoes, scrubbed

1 cup water

A pinch of salt and black pepper

½ teaspoon smoked paprika

½ teaspoon cumin, ground

Directions:

Put the water in your pressure cooker, add the steamer basket, add sweet potatoes inside, cover and cook on High for 10 minutes.

Split potatoes, add salt, pepper, paprika and cumin, divide them between plates and serve as a side dish.

Nutrition: calories 152, fat 2, fiber 3, carbs 4, protein 4

18. Broccoli Pasta

Preparation time: 10 minutes

Cooking time: 4 minutes

Servings: 2

Ingredients:

2 cups water

½ pound pasta

8 ounces cheddar cheese, grated

½ cup broccoli

½ cup half and half

Directions:

Put the water and the pasta in your pressure cooker.

Add the steamer basket, add the broccoli, cover the cooker and cook on High for 4 minutes.

Drain pasta, transfer it as well as the broccoli, and clean the pot.

Set it on sauté mode, add pasta and broccoli, cheese and half and half, stir well, cook for 2 minutes, divide between plates and serve as a side dish for chicken.

Nutrition: calories 211, fat 4, fiber 2, carbs 6, protein 7

19. Cauliflower Rice

Preparation time: 10 minutes

Cooking time: 12 minutes

Servings: 2

 Ingredients:

1 tablespoon olive oil

½ cauliflower head, florets separated

A pinch of salt and black pepper

A pinch of parsley flakes

¼ teaspoon cumin, ground

¼ teaspoon turmeric powder

¼ teaspoon paprika

1 cup water

½ tablespoon cilantro, chopped

Juice from 1/3 lime

Directions:

Put the water in your pressure cooker, add the steamer basket, add cauliflower florets, cover and cook on High for 2 minutes.

Discard water, transfer cauliflower to a plate and leave aside.

Clean your pressure cooker, add the oil, set on sauté mode and heat it up.

Add cauliflower, mash using a potato masher, add salt, pepper, parsley, cumin, turmeric, paprika, cilantro and lime juice, stir well, cook for 10 minutes more, divide between 2 plates and serve as a side dish.

Nutrition: calories 191, fat 1, fiber 2, carbs 4, protein 5

20. Refried Beans

Preparation time: 10 minutes

Cooking time: 35 minutes

Servings: 2

Ingredients:

1 pound pinto beans, soaked for 20 minutes and drained

1 cup onion, chopped

2 garlic cloves, minced

1 teaspoon oregano, dried

½ jalapeno, chopped

1 teaspoon cumin, ground

A pinch of salt and black pepper

1 and ½ tablespoon olive oil

2 cups chicken stock

Directions:

In your pressure cooker, mix oil with onion, jalapeno, garlic, oregano, cumin, salt, pepper, stock and beans, stir, cover and cook on Manual for 30 minutes.

Stir beans one more time, divide them between 2 plates and serve as a side dish.

Nutrition: calories 200, fat 1, fiber 3, carbs 7, protein 7

Dessert Recipes

21. Carrots bread

Preparation time: 10 minutes

Cooking time: 40 minutes

Servings: 6

Ingredients:

2 cups carrots, peeled and grated

1 cup sugar

3 eggs, whisked

2 cups white flour

1 tablespoon baking soda

1 cup almond milk

Directions:

In a bowl, combine the carrots with the sugar and the other ingredients, whisk well, pour this into a lined loaf pan, introduce the pan in the air fryer and cook at 340 degrees f for 40 minutes.

Cool the bread down, slice and serve.

Nutrition: calories 200, fat 5, fiber 3, carbs 13, protein 7

22. Pear pudding

Preparation time: 10 minutes

Cooking time: 20 minutes

Servings: 6

Ingredients:

3 tablespoons sugar

½ cup butter, melted

2 eggs, whisked

2 pears, peeled and chopped

1/3 cup almond milk

½ cup heavy cream

Directions:

In a bowl, combine the butter with the sugar and the other ingredients, whisk well and pour into a pudding pan.

Introduce the pan in the air fryer and cook at 340 degrees f for 20 minutes.

Cool the pudding down, divide into bowls and serve.

Nutrition: calories 211, fat 4, fiber 6, carbs 14, protein 6

Vegetarian Recipes

23. Broccoli and Almonds

Preparation Time: 5 minutes

Cooking Time: 12 minutes

Servings: 4

Ingredients:

1 lb. broccoli florets

½ cup almonds; chopped

3 garlic cloves; minced

1 tbsp. chives; chopped

2 tbsp. red vinegar

3 tbsp. coconut oil; melted

A pinch of salt and black pepper

Directions:

Take a bowl and mix the broccoli with the garlic, salt, pepper, vinegar and the oil and toss.

Put the broccoli in your air fryer's basket and cook at 380°F for 12 minutes

Divide between plates and serve with almonds and chives sprinkled on top.

Nutrition: Calories: 180; Fat: 4g; Fiber: 2g; Carbs: 4g; Protein: 6g

24. Turmeric Cabbage

Preparation Time: 5 minutes

Cooking Time: 15 minutes

Servings: 4

Ingredients:

1 green cabbage head, shredded

¼ cup ghee; melted

1 tbsp. dill; chopped.

2 tsp. turmeric powder

Directions:

In a pan that fits your air fryer, mix the cabbage with the rest of the ingredients except the dill, toss, put the pan in the fryer and cook at 370°F for 15 minutes

Divide everything between plates and serve with dill sprinkled on top.

Nutrition: Calories: 173; Fat: 5g; Fiber: 3g; Carbs: 6g; Protein: 7g

25. Spicy Cauliflower Rice

Preparation Time: 10 minutes

Cooking Time: 22 minutes

Servings: 2

Ingredients:

1 cauliflower head, cut into florets

1/2 tsp cumin

1/2 tsp chili powder

6 onion spring, chopped

2 jalapenos, chopped

4 tbsp olive oil

1 zucchini, trimmed and cut into cubes

1/2 tsp paprika

1/2 tsp garlic powder

1/2 tsp cayenne pepper

1/2 tsp pepper

1/2 tsp salt

Directions:

Preheat the air fryer to 370 F.

Add cauliflower florets into the food processor and process

until it looks like rice.

Transfer cauliflower rice into the air fryer baking pan and drizzle with half oil.

Place pan in the air fryer and cook for 12 minutes, stir halfway through.

Heat remaining oil in a small pan over medium heat.

Add zucchini and cook for 5-8 minutes.

Add onion and jalapenos and cook for 5 minutes.

Add spices and stir well. Set aside.

Add cauliflower rice in the zucchini mixture and stir well.

Serve and enjoy.

Nutrition:

Calories 254

Fat 28 g

Carbohydrates 12.3 g

Sugar 5 g

Protein 4.3 g

Cholesterol 0 mg

26. Broccoli Stuffed Peppers

Preparation Time: 10 minutes

Cooking Time: 40 minutes

Servings: 2

Ingredients:

4 eggs

1/2 cup cheddar cheese, grated

2 bell peppers, cut in half and remove seeds

1/2 tsp garlic powder

1 tsp dried thyme

1/4 cup feta cheese, crumbled

1/2 cup broccoli, cooked

1/4 tsp pepper

1/2 tsp salt

Directions:

Preheat the air fryer to 325 F.

Stuff feta and broccoli into the bell peppers halved.

Beat egg in a bowl with seasoning and pour egg mixture into the pepper halved over feta and broccoli.

Place bell pepper halved into the air fryer basket and cook for 35-40 minutes.

Top with grated cheddar cheese and cook until cheese melted.

Serve and enjoy.

Nutrition:

Calories 340

Fat 22 g

Carbohydrates 12 g

Sugar 8.2 g

Protein 22 g

Cholesterol 374 mg

27. Zucchini Muffins

Preparation Time: 10 minutes

Cooking Time: 20 minutes

Servings: 8

Ingredients:

6 eggs

4 drops stevia

1/4 cup Swerve

1/3 cup coconut oil, melted

1 cup zucchini, grated

3/4 cup coconut flour

1/4 tsp ground nutmeg

1 tsp ground cinnamon

1/2 tsp baking soda

Directions:

Preheat the air fryer to 325 F.

Add all ingredients except zucchini in a bowl and mix well.

Add zucchini and stir well.

Pour batter into the silicone muffin molds and place into the air fryer basket.

Cook muffins for 20 minutes.

Serve and enjoy.

Nutrition:

Calories 136

Fat 12 g

Carbohydrates 1 g

Sugar 0.6 g

Protein 4 g

Cholesterol 123 mg

28. Herbed Duck Legs

Preparation Time: 10 minutes

Cooking Time: 30 minutes

Servings: 2

Ingredients

1 garlic clove, minced

½ tablespoon fresh thyme, chopped

½ tablespoon fresh parsley, chopped

1 teaspoon five spice powder

Salt and ground black pepper, as required

2 duck legs

Directions

Set the temperature of air fryer to 340 degrees F. Grease an air fryer basket.

In a bowl, mix together the garlic, herbs, five spice powder, salt, and black pepper.

Generously rub the duck legs with garlic mixture.

Arrange duck legs into the prepared air fryer basket.

Air fry for about 25 minutes and then 5 more minutes at 390 degrees F.

Remove from air fryer and place the duck legs onto the serving platter.

Serve hot.

Nutrition

Calories: 138

Carbohydrate: 1g

Protein: 25g

Fat: 4.5g

Sugar: 0g

Sodium: 82mg

29. Easy Rib Eye Steak

Preparation Time: 10 minutes

Cooking Time: 14 minutes

 Servings: 4

Ingredients

2 lbs. rib eye steak

1 tablespoon olive oil

1 tablespoon steak rub*

Directions

Set the temperature of air fryer to 400 degrees F. Grease an air fryer basket.

Coat the steak with oil and then, generously rub with steak rub.

Place steak into the prepared air fryer basket.

Air fry for about 14 minutes, flipping once halfway through.

Remove from air fryer and place the steak onto a cutting board for about 10 minutes before slicing.

Cut the steak into desired size slices and transfer onto serving plates.

Serve immediately.

Nutrition

Calories: 438

Carbohydrate: 0g

Protein: 26.88g

Fat: 35.8g

Sugar: 0g

Sodium: 157mg

Air fryer Bonus Recipes

1. Air Fryer Sausage Patties

Prep Time 2 minutes Total Time 10 minutes,

Air Fryer Sausage Patties, Breakfast Sausage Air Fryer
Servings: 1 Calorie: 142 kcal **Ingredients**

- (Sausage links or patties)
- 1 Serving Breakfast Sausage (1.5 ounces/43 grams)

Blend with your favorite sauce.

Cut or shape the sausage into 1/4 "balls, and place it in the
air fryer bowl.

Cook at 400 degrees for 8–10 minutes, turning on halfway.

Breakfast Cuisine: American

Boiled Eggs

Servings for: six eggs Calories: 78 kcal

Ingredients

- Six eggs
- Oil Spritz, on chickens, so they don't fall together.

Instructions

Put in the air fryer the wire rack or egg adapter that came
with your air fryer or accessory kit.

Place all six eggs with string onto the shelf. When two eggs touch each other, they softly oil the eggs, as they stay together—Cook at 250 temperature for 18 to 20 minutes. Remove the eggs and put them in an ice-water pan. Peel, cook, and eat your snack.

2. Air Fryer Breakfast Potatoes

Breakfast

Cuisine: American

Keyword: Air Fried Breakfast Potatoes, Servings: 4

Calories: 180 kcal

Ingredients

- 2-3 big potatoes can also use 1/2 bag of frozen diced potatoes to save time
- One onion, diced
- One red pepper, diced 1 tsp.
- Garlic paste with 1/2 tsp.
- One Teaspoon of paprika.
- One teaspoon water.
- And Spritz Your Favorite Oil

Instructions

Mix in a large bowl with all ingredients. (Simply spray the mixture until the correct quantity of oil is exceeded by using an oil mister.) Spritz the base of the air fryer basket to prevent damage, or using a filter.

Place the potatoes inside the air-fryer bowl.

Cook at 390 degrees for 15–20 minutes, stirring at frequent intervals.

3. Apple Baked by Air Fryer

In this world, your handmade apple granola or favorite cereal couldn't top this unbelievably sweet, sinuously delightful Apple Baked by Air Fryer.

This kind of recipe is the best possible way to turn pure and basic elements into totally indistinctive thing. These kinds of appliances are a blessing from above that makes it possible to receive fat, caramelized, and soft therapies, independent of the aim of weight loss.

All that you require is simply a shred of cinnamon and butter. This recipe for Apple baking is kind of American classic sure to add warmth to your style without crashing the bank with calories. Apple Baked by Air Fryer officially clocks under 150 calories (including Smart Carb variety carbohydrates), which carry the bakery flavor to a few of your preferred calorie-loaded baked goods. Why do you want apples to consider now? For a flex meal get up.

For two serving, per serving calories is 139, Register as one-half SmartCarb, one-half Power Oil, and one **Additional Ingredient:**

- One average Pear or Apple

- Two spoons Walnuts.

- Two tbsp. small raisins

- Dark margarine, one and half tsp. melted.

- 1/4 tsp. cinnamon.

- Nutmeg 1/4 cup water

Guidance:

• Heat the fryer to 350 ° Fahrenheit in advance.

Instructions:

Slice the pear or apple about the center in half, and spoon some flesh out.

Put the pear or apple in the saucepan (air fryer component) or in the base of the air fryer (after the attachment is removed).

Combine a small cup of margarine, sugar, nutmeg, raisins and walnut.

Put this mix into halve centers of apple or pear.

Put water inside the casserole.

Bake 20 more minutes.

4. Air Fryer Cinnamon Rolls

The tasty little cinnamon rolls will bake in just 10 minutes AND have an alternate grocery use store-bought bread dough as the basis. Of course, if you want to make the dough from scratch, then that's always good!

Time for preparation: 20 McCook Time: 9 minutes Total time: 29 servings: 8

Ingredients to be added

- One pound of frozen bread flour,
- One-fourth cup of cooled and melted butter
- Three-fourth cup of sugar (Brown)
- One and half spoon of cinnamon (Ground)
- Coat of cream cheese
- Smoothed 4 ounces of cream cheese
- 2 tbsp. Butter, smooth
- 1 1/4 cups of powdered sugar
- 1/2 tablespoon of vanilla directions. Now, allow the bread to spread in a thirteen-inch triangle of eleven inch on a gently floured surface. Place the rectangle in front of the thirteen-inch foot. Brush the molten

butter across the bottom of the pastry, remaining one-inch edge exposed farthest from you.

Instructions

Within a shallow pot, add the cinnamon and brown sugar. Sprinkle onto buttered bread the mixture uniformly and reveal the one-inch side. Enfold the bread into shape of log beginning at the bottom nearest to you. Enfold the bread firmly, making sure that it spreads uniformly, pushing out any pockets of air. Put pressure on the bread onto the wraps to tie it together until you reach the uncovered bottom of the dough.

Cut the log into eight pieces, slice the bread gently with a gesture to saw, so you don't flatten it. Flip the upside-down slices and cover them with a neat cloth. Now let wraps sit for sixty to eighty min in the moderately hot area of your kitchen.

Put the butter and cream cheese in an oven to make the coating. Soften the paste inside the oven for thirty sec at a moment, so it is fast to blend. Add the sugar in powdered form bit by bit, then mix to blend. Now add the whisk and vanilla extract till smoothness. Now keep it separately.

Once the wraps have grown, Heat the fryer in advance till 350 Fahrenheit.

Shift 4 of the wraps into fryer's bucket. Switch the wraps over fifteen-minute air-cook, and cook for another four minutes. Match with four remaining wraps.

Now, Let the wraps chill down for some time until the coating. Put a large coating of cream cheese over mild hot cinnamon wraps, causing a little of the coating to spill down the border of the wraps. Serve a little hot, and be delighted!

5. Cranberry Pecan Muffins (Gluten-Free) Air Fryer Recipe

An easy blender recipe for weekend brunch or breakfast that serves cranberry pecan muffins (gluten-free) every day. These muffins are fried in the air fryer and take about 15 minutes to bake Fast during the fall and winter months, and other baked goods contain Simple Cranberries.

We don't always need to limit cranberry baking to falling and winter months. Cookies and muffins containing fresh cranberries can be used at any time of year. If fresh cranberries are out of season, a frozen bag of cranberries is still available for collection.

To be honest, I've just used fresh cranberries a couple of times up to this year. I dove into the cranberry bog this year and made several muffins with fresh cranberries and a fast sandwich.

Sure, they were utterly irresistible— the well-baked cranberries adding a sweet tartness. If you need to chill in the afternoon, make a cup of tea and savor this gluten-free cranberry pecan muffins air fryer recipe.

For example, muffins are great for breakfast at every time of year. This is a recipe for a blender means you can cook up this dish in no time. Let's bake instead!

Prep Time: 15 minutes

Bake Time 10 minutes or less:

Total Time: 25-35 min.

Yield: 6-8 muffins

Cooking: Muffins

Ingredients

- 1/4 cup of cashew milk (or use whatever milk you prefer)
- Two big eggs
- 1/2 tsp. of vanilla essence.
- 1 1/2 cup Almond Flour
- 1/4 cup Monk fruit extract (or using your favorite sweetener)
- 1 tsp. baking powder.
- Cinnamon: 1/4 tsp.
- 1/8 tsp. Salt
- 1/2 cup fresh cranberries
- 1/4 cup chopped pecans

Instructions

Try adding the milk, eggs, and vanilla extract to the mixer and blend for 20-30 seconds together.

In the almond – mix for another 30-45 seconds, add the flour, sugar, baking powder, cinnamon, and salt until well mixed.

Remove the blender jar off the foundation and mix in 1/2 the fresh cranberries and pecans. Transfer the mixture to silicone muffin cups. Finish each of the muffins with some remaining fresh cranberries.

Place the muffins in the air-fryer basket and bake on 325- or for 12-15 minutes until the toothpick is clean.

Lift from the air fryer and cool on the wire rack.

Drizzle with a maple glaze where possible. The melted white chocolate is also drizzled over some of the muffins, bake in a preheated 325-degree oven for twenty-five to thirty minutes for Oven Baking, or until a toothpick comes out clean.

6. Air Fryer Strawberry Pop-Tarts

Maybe the best invention is still Air Fryer Baked Pop-Tarts of Raspberry! Almost all of you probably recall Pop-Tarts. Well, few of you could even eat or feed Pop-Tarts to your kids. We all have sentimental recollection from our early years, which include Pop-Tarts. Our moms often bought the cinnamon essence variety, for some excuse. We have nothing about cinnamon, but a kid's strawberry flavor tastes unusually great!

Total calories are 274 with fat equal to 14 grams along with carbs equal to 32 grams and protein equal to 3 grams. Handmade Pop-Tarts of Strawberry in air fryer is a fast and simple nutritious meal for cream cheese with low fat, stevia and Greek vanilla yogurt added sugar-free frosting. To adults a child-friendly meal is great as well!

Preparation Time is ten min and Total Time is twenty-five min top for the servings of six individuals, this meal has total of 274 kilo calories.

Ingredients

- Two cooled pie crusts
- One table spoon of cornstarch

- One-third cup of preserved strawberry with low sugar.
- Half cup of simple, non-fat Greek vanilla yogurt I used a cutting board made of bamboo.

Instructions:

Slice the two pie crusts into six rectangles, by using a pizza cutter or knife (From each pie crust three). Growing to surround the pop-tart will be fairly lengthy until you turn it around.

Place the cornstarch and preserves in a pot, then mix well.

Drop a spoonful of preserves onto the crust and put the preserves on the crust's top.

To save, fold the pop-tarts over each, using a fork to create horizontal and vertical lines around the sides and create sensations of each of the pop-tarts.

Now put the pop-tarts in Air Fryer. Sprinkle on grease. I want to use the olive oil.

Please bake at 375 Fahrenheit for at least ten min also you will to examine the pop-tarts for about eight min to make sure they're not too crisp to your liking.

Bring together stevia, Greek yogurt and cream cheese in a tub to make the frosting.

Enable the pop-tarts to chill down before removing the fryer. Well it is really crucial. Unless you don't let them cool off, then they could crack. Drop Pop-Tart from the fryer. Cover each with frosting. Sprinkle of sugar over the sprinkles.

Recommended baking two to three pop-tarts at single time in fryer. As you may pile them up, also they will separate finely until they've completely cooled up. Though not adding them to ensure delivery works best.

7. Peanut Butter and Jelly Air Fried Doughnuts

Look at those light, fluffy doughnuts, oozing jam, and dripping peanut butter glaze? New from the fryer! To air fryers, such beauties are a wonder.

Ingredients (6 Doughnuts):

- 1 1/4 cups of all-purpose flour
- 1/3 cup of sugar
- 1/2 teaspoon baking powder
- 1/2 teaspoon baking soda
- 3/4 teaspoon salt
- 1 Egg
- 1/2 cup buttermilk
- One teaspoon vanilla
- Two tablespoons of unsalted butter which should be melted and cooled
- One tablespoon melted butter to clean the tops

Filling: • 1/2 cup Blueberry or raspberry jelly (not preserved)

Instructions:

Build a well in the middle of the dry product, then spill the water. Mix with a fork, and finish mixing with a large spoon before the flour is added.

Turn the dough out into a well-floured sheet. Mind this would be very sticky at first. Perform the dough very slowly until it reaches a 3/4 "thickness and then pat it out, Using a 3 1/2 "knife to remove the dough circles and to wipe the melting butter. Try to Cut out 2 "pieces of parchment paper (doesn't need to be precise) and put each dough round on the board, then in the air fryer. Act in loads depending on how many you can fit inside your fryer. Fry at 350 degrees for 11 minutes, using a squeeze bottle or pastry container, each doughnut can fill with jelly.

8. Blueberry Lemon Muffins

Training Time: 5-8 minutes. Cook Hour: 10-12 min.

Average time: 25-35 min.

Cuisine: American

Ingredients:

- 2 1/2 cups of self-rising flour

- 1/2 cup of monk fruit (or using your choice sugar)

- 1/2 cup of milk

- 1/4 cup of avocado oil (any soft cooking oil)

- Two eggs

- 1 cup of blueberries

- One lemon zest

- One lemon juice

- 1 tsp. Vanilla

- Brown topping sugar (a little sprinkling on top of each muffin-less than a teaspoon) Direction Mix the self-growing flour and sugar. Set aside in a small bowl.
  Layer milk, sugar, lemon juice, bacon, and coffee in a small saucepan

Instructions:

Attach the flour mixture to the liquid mixture and stir in the blueberries until combined.

In silicone cupcake cups, spoon the batter, sprinkle 1/2 tsp. — brown sugar on top of each muffin;

Bake for 10 minutes at 320 degrees; check the muffins at 6 minutes to ensure that they do not cook too quickly. Place one toothpick in the center of a muffin, and it ends until the toothpick comes out clean and the muffins brown. No need to over-bake the muffins; once they are removed from the air fryer, they can carry on to cook for another minute or two.

Remove and make it new.

This dish can also be cooked on the oven for 12-15 minutes at 350 degrees.

Put all these in a plastic bag and refrigerate if you have extra muffins. They're going to live 4-5 days, new. When they are ready to eat, seal the muffin tightly in a paper towel and cook for 10 seconds in the microwave. Serve with a big glass of milk, coffee, tea or hot cocoa,

9. Air Fryer French toast Soldiers

You will have to go with lots of troops, and two wonderful soft boiled eggs. They were good, and because of the egg factor and the kick of the carbs, that will leave you complete for hours and hours.

While this isn't everyone's cup of tea, the mixture of eggs and breakfast bread has always been a great one.

You drip the bread into an egg and then prepare it outside with a tasty coating of butter. So you do so, however much you want. And a good Berries seasoning!!!

This recipe (which is really simple to make) takes just a few minutes and makes the ideal breakfast to set you up for the day.

Prep Time 5 mins Cook Time 10 mins Total Time 15 mins Servings: 2

Ingredients:

- 4 Slices of Full Meal Bread
- 2 Broad Eggs
- 1/4 Cup Whole Milk
- 1/4 Cup Brown Sugar

- 1 Tbsp. Honey

- 1 Tsp. Cinnamon

- Nutmeg pinch

- Icing Sugar pinch

Instructions

Cut up the bread slices into troops. Any soldiers slice will make 4.

Put the remaining ingredients in a mixing bowl (except icing sugar), then blend properly.

Dip each soldier into the mixture to well cover the mixture and put it in the Air Fryer. Once you're done, you'll have 16 soldiers, and so everyone will be warm and soaked from the mix.

Put on 160c for 10 minutes, or until the toast is crispy and cool and not sticky anymore. By cooking, turn them over halfway so that both sides of the soldiers have a fair chance to cook equally.

Serve with some new berries and a swirl of icing sugar.

In this chapter, we will present air fryer recipes of main course meals for lunches.

10. Chimichurri Steak

Active: fifteen minutes total: 35 minutes serves: 2

Ingredients:

For chimichurri

- One-pound skirt steak

- One cup parsley, finely chopped

- One-fourth cup of basil, finely chopped

- Two tea-spoon of oregano, finely chopped

- Three garlic cloves, finely chopped

- One tea-spoon of red pepper

- One tea-spoon of cumin

- One tea-spoon of cayenne pepper

- One tea-spoon of black pepper

- One-fourth cup of olive oil

Instructions:

1. Combine the Chimichurri ingredients into a mixing pot. Cut the steak into two 8-ounce portions, and add the chimichurri 1/4 cup to a re-sealable jar. Refrigerate after 24 hours for 2 hours. Switch from the fridge 30 minutes before cooking.

2. Air fryer preheat to 390 ° F. Pat dry steak with a towel made from rubber. Attach the steak to the pot, and prep for medium-rare for 8-10 minutes.

3. Garnish with 2 Chimichurri tablespoons on top and serve.

11. Roasted Heirloom Tomato with Baked Feta

Active: twenty minutes total: 35 minutes serves: 4

Ingredients:

For the tomato

- One heirloom tomato
- One 8-ounce block of feta cheese
- Half cup of red onions
- One tablespoon of olive oil
- One pinch of salt

For the basil pesto

- 1/2 cup of parsley, finely chopped
- 1/2 cup of parmesan cheese, rubbed
- Three tablespoons of pine nuts, toasted
- One garlic clove
- olive oil
- One pinch of salt

Instructions:

1. Make pesto. Attach the parsley, spinach, parmesan, garlic, toast pine nuts, and salt in a food processor.

2. Switch on the food processor, and apply the olive oil gradually. Store and refrigerate until ready to use, once all the olive oil is mixed into the pesto.

3. 2. Air fryer preheat to 390 ° F. Break the tomato and feta into thin slices, 1/2 inch long.

4. With a paper towel, dry the tomato. Place one spoonful of pesto on top of each slice of tomatoes and finish with the feta. Throw the red onions with one spoonful of olive oil and put them on top of the feta.

5. Place the tomatoes/feta in the basket and cook for 12-14 minutes or until the feta begins softening and browning. Finish off with a tablespoon of salt and an extra basil pesto spoonful.

Lightning Source UK Ltd.
Milton Keynes UK
UKHW021017240621
386074UK00004B/240